# The King and the Ship

and

# The Quiz

PHASE 3

/sh/th/ng/

Level 3 – Yellow

# Helpful Hints for Reading at Home

**The graphemes (written letters) and phonemes (units of sound) used throughout this series are aligned with Letters and Sounds. This offers a consistent approach to learning whether reading at home or in the classroom.**

**HERE IS A LIST OF PHONEMES FOR THIS PHASE OF LEARNING. AN EXAMPLE OF THE PRONUNCIATION CAN BE FOUND IN BRACKETS.**

| Phase 3 | | | |
|---|---|---|---|
| j (jug) | v (van) | w (wet) | x (fox) |
| y (yellow) | z (zoo) | zz (buzz) | qu (quick) |
| ch (chip) | sh (shop) | th (thin/then) | ng (ring) |
| ai (rain) | ee (feet) | igh (night) | oa (boat) |
| oo (boot/look) | ar (farm) | or (for) | ur (hurt) |
| ow (cow) | oi (coin) | ear (dear) | air (fair) |
| ure (sure) | er (corner) | | |

**HERE ARE SOME WORDS WHICH YOUR CHILD MAY FIND TRICKY.**

| Phase 3 Tricky Words | | | |
|---|---|---|---|
| he | you | she | they |
| we | all | me | are |
| be | my | was | her |

GPC focus: /sh/th/ng/

## TOP TIPS FOR HELPING YOUR CHILD TO READ:

- Allow children time to break down unfamiliar words into units of sound and then encourage children to string these sounds together to create the word.
- Encourage your child to point out any focus phonics when they are used.
- Read through the book more than once to grow confidence.
- Ask simple questions about the text to assess understanding.
- Encourage children to use illustrations as prompts.

PHASE 3

/sh/th/ng/

This book focuses on the phonemes /sh/, /th/ and /ng/ and is a yellow level 3 book band.

# The King and the Ship

and

# The Quiz

**Written by**
Georgie Tennant

**Illustrated by**
Lynne Feng

Can you say this sound and draw it with your finger?

# The King and the Ship

**Written by**
Georgie Tennant

**Illustrated by**
Lynne Feng

King Zack is on his ship. It hit a rock.

"No! The ship has a rip in it," King Zack yells.

It has hit this big rock. It is a shock.

King Zack gets off the ship. He is sad.

He zigzags up a long path with his bag.

"I will fix this ship!" King Zack yells.

Look at this. It is a shell.

It is a bit dull. King Zack rubs the shell.

"Tell me a wish," sings the shell.
Zack gets a shock.

Zack zigzags back up the path with the shell.

"I wish there was not a rip in it!" he yells.

King Zack is on his ship. It can go!

Can you say this sound and draw it with your finger?

# The Quiz

**Written by**
Georgie Tennant

**Illustrated by**
Lynne Feng

Ben and Sam go to a quiz.

They can win this cash. It is a big sum.

"Ding if you can tell me what this is."

"What has legs and then has wings?"
Ding! "A moth!"

"What is thick but can be thin?"
Ding! "A shell!"

"What can dash and hiss and run?"
Ding! "A cat!"

Sam is sad that he cannot win the cash.

"What can rip a ship?"

Ben lets Sam go.
Ding! "A big rock!" "Yes!"

"What can sell rabbits and cats?"
Ding! "A pet shop!"

"What can fill up and be fun?"
Ding! "A bath!"

"We win the cash!" yell Ben and Sam.

King's Lynn, Norfolk PE30 4LS

ISBN 978-1-83927-440-4

Printed in Malaysia.
A catalogue record for this book is available from the British Library.

**The King and the Ship & The Quiz**
Written by Georgie Tennant
Illustrated by Lynne Feng

# An Introduction to BookLife Readers...

**Our Readers have been specifically created in line with the London Institute of Education's approach to book banding and are phonetically decodable and ordered to support each phase of Letters and Sounds.**

Each book has been created to provide the best possible reading and learning experience. Our aim is to share our love of books with children, providing both emerging readers and prolific page-turners with beautiful books that are guaranteed to provoke interest and learning, regardless of ability.

**BOOK BAND GRADED** using the Institute of Education's approach to levelling.

**PHONETICALLY DECODABLE** supporting each phase of Letters and Sounds.

**EXERCISES AND QUESTIONS** to offer reinforcement and to ascertain comprehension.

**BEAUTIFULLY ILLUSTRATED** to inspire and provoke engagement, providing a variety of styles for the reader to enjoy whilst reading through the series.

## AUTHOR INSIGHT:
## GEORGIE TENNANT

Georgie Tennant is a freelance writer who has written multiple stories for BookLife Publishing. She always knew she would be a writer as she used to present her school teachers with lengthy stories and poems for them to enjoy! Her two sons provide plenty of entertaining material for her writing, which usually appears on her blog or in the local newspaper as the 'Thought for the Week'. When she isn't writing she is working as a part-time secondary school English teacher, where she has the joy of inspiring slightly bigger children with the joy of reading good stories. She hopes to write good stories for them one day too.

PHASE 3

/sh/th/ng/

This book focuses on the phonemes /sh/, /th/ and /ng/ and is a yellow level 3 book band.